American Indian Freemasonry

By Arthur C. Parker, 32°
Foreword for the 2024 edition by Michael R. Poll

CORNERSTONE EDITION

Cornerstone Book Publishers
Hot Springs Village, AR
2024

American Indian Freemasonry
By Arthur C. Parker
Foreword by Michael R. Poll

A Cornerstone Book
Published by Cornerstone Book Publishers

Copyright © 2013 & 2024 by Cornerstone Book Publishers

All rights reserved under International and Pan-American Copyright Conventions. No part of this book may be reproduced in any manner without permission in writing from the copyright holder, except by a reviewer, who may quote brief passages in a review.

Cornerstone Book Publishers
Hot Springs Village, AR
www.cornerstonepublishers.com

Originally Published -1919

First Cornerstone Edition - 2013
Second Cornerstone Edition - 2024

ISBN: 979-8-3481-0839-7

DEDICATION

To Ga-je-wa, Ho-doin-jai-ey and Ho-skwi-sa-onh, three friends who have done most to lead me on in the journey where I have received more light in Masonry, and whose brotherly love and affection have demonstrated to many a wayfarer the potency of the Masonic tie, this account of American Indian Freemasonry is dedicated, by their friend

GA-WA-SO-WA-NEH

Table of Contents

Foreword xi

American Indian Freemasonry 1

Is There an Undiscovered Masonry? 5

What Is Freemasonry? 7

What Is the Natural Masonry of the Red Man? 9

How Did American Indian Freemasonry Originate? 14

Was the Red Man a Craftsman and Builder? 17

What Was the Red Man's Religious Life? 19

What Happened? 25

Red Hand, The Brother-Friend 27

The Promise of Power 31

Out of the Darkness 34

Da-Ne-Hoh. What Has Happened Has Happened. 36

A Practical Postscript 38

In the beginning God created heaven and earth. ~ *Genesis*.
Remove not the ancient landmark which thy fathers have *set*.
~ *Solomon*.

Speculative masonry is so far interwoven with religion as to lay us under the strongest obligations to pay that rational homage to the Deity, which at once constitutes our duty and our happiness. It leads the contemplative to view with reverence and admiration the glorious works of creation and inspires them with the most exalted ideas of the perfection of the divine Creator.
~ *Samuel Cole*.

We also have a religion which was given to our forefathers and has been handed down from father to son. We worship in that way. It teaches us to be thankful for all the favors we receive, to love one another and be united.
~ *Red Jacket*.

It is more than probable that the diversified customs, institutions and religions of the several nations of the world are less dissimilar in their origin than is often imagined. The differences arose in the progress of time, the shifting scenes of climate, condition and event. But the original ideas of existence and the laws that pertain to all created things are pretty much the same among all the tribes of mankind.
~ *Westropp, Ancient Symbol Worship*

To The Iroquois

Beautiful thy meditations
In thy consecrated forests,
Fragrant in their odorous incense
When,—though groping in the darkness, —
Thou wert lifted up and strengthened,
In thy earnest firm endeavor,
Nearer drawn to one Great Spirit
In thy ardor of devotion!
~ *Converse.*

Foreword

As a young boy, I loved to go to a nearby open field and fly my kite. I enjoyed seeing it soar up in the sky. One day, another boy came to the field to fly his kite alongside me. Before long, the kites came too close to each other and became tangled. It was a mess.

A few weeks later, I went to the field again to fly my kite. After a short time, I saw another boy coming to the field with a kite. Remembering my event a few weeks prior, I was not happy to see him. I wanted him to find another place to fly his kite. For some reason, I didn't want to rehash the story of the tangled kites, so I yelled out, "Hey, you can't fly your kite here. I own all the wind in this field!" My grandfather was over on the side and heard me. He broke out laughing. "How in the world does anyone *own* the wind?" he asked with a smile. I realized how foolish I sounded and didn't pursue the nonsensical claim.

Over the years, I have thought about my childish claim. How could anyone own anything like the wind, the clouds, laughter, kindness, anger, or any such thing? They can't. The elements and emotions defy the very nature of ownership. In fact, the concept of *ownership* of many things can conflict with many established rules of fairness, morality, and logic. Let's look at it.

Let's say I am sitting in front of a warm fire on a cold winter night. I begin to think about how comfortable I feel in front of that nice, warm fire. Those are *my* thoughts. But what if someone else is in the same situation and feels the same thing? Can he say these are *his* thoughts when they are exactly the same as *mine*? Can I claim ownership of that thought? Can we really *own* thoughts and feelings? It's nonsense to say I feel good, but you can't feel good, too, because I *own* that feeling. This *ownership* concept can get out of hand. There is a difference between owning something and experiencing something.

And this all brings us to Freemasonry. Does anyone *own* Freemasonry? Well, I guess that depends on how you define it. If you define Freemasonry as an organization, then ownership of Masonic organizations is often claimed. Various organizations calling themselves "Freemasonry" have organized themselves and even registered as state corporations. In the eyes of our civil law, they are recognized as legitimate organizations of Freemasonry. However, in the eyes of Masonic Grand Lodges (organizations themselves), these other organizations may or may not be recognized as legitimate Masonic organizations, regardless of what our civil law says. Masonic Grand Lodges make their own rules. Additionally, individual Masons may not always be aware of how different bodies of Freemasonry are viewed. Individual Masons may also not be aware of *why* some organizations are determined to be legitimate, and others are not. Legitimacy and *ownership* can sometimes be a bit cloudy.

There is, however, another aspect to Freemasonry that is important to understand. Freemasonry is of a dual nature. It is an organization, but it is also a philosophy. It is an ancient philosophy teaching symbolic lessons of morality and self-improvement. It is undoubtedly far older than the established dates we have of the various organizations of Speculative

Freemasonry. We can find traces of these emblematic teachings in the very early days of humanity. The ancient Egyptian Legend of Osiris is a symbolic story/lesson predating the commonly accepted age of Speculative Freemasonry. We can find similar examples of these sorts of teachings in all corners of the globe. So, who *owns* the philosophy and symbolic lessons used by Freemasonry? I believe that this is the same as asking who owns the wind.

The symbolic lessons used by Freemasonry cannot be owned (by our common understanding of ownership) by anyone. Still, they can be experienced and embraced by those who understand and accept those teachings. Freemasonry teaches Universal Truths that have been received and taught by people in all corners of the world from time immemorial. Read this book. The similarities between what is taught in the Native American schools of initiation and Freemasonry are apparent. We come from the same source. And what is that source? Look to the most profound lessons, and you will understand.

As an organization, Freemasonry is limited to the quality of any club. But as a moral philosophy, Freemasonry soars like an eagle to the highest mountains of spiritual enlightenment. I view the philosophy of Freemasonry as our physical guide to an everlasting spiritual life. It is the property of no one. It is available to anyone with the ability to grow.

Michael R. Poll
2024

American Indian Freemasonry

A tall bronze-skinned guide led the way over an ice-rutted road. The journey toward the mysterious East had commenced. Following the guide in single file were four, but really three—for one was the conductor, in whose presence the three were assured safety from all danger not of their own making. In all, there were five, and such is the order of the journey.

It was in the land of the Senecas, those most powerful confederates of the famous Six Nations of the Iroquois. To this land in the Valley of the Cattaraugus had journeyed the Commander-in-Chief of Buffalo Consistory with three other members of the Ancient Accepted Scottish Rite of Masonry. The time was midwinter on the moon of Nis-ko-wuk-ni, the appointed time when the great Thanksgiving of the Senecas takes place in a nine-day celebration. During this season of gratitude to the Great Spirit, the various fraternities and ceremonial associations hold sessions, and a few of them give public exhibitions. Not so, however, with one whose work is all secret and into whose chamber only those purified and loyal are admitted.

The guide led on and the four followed, three being candidates for initiation. The glimmering light held by the guide cast an uncertain ray upon the trail that penetrated the moonless winter night. It was not an easy path nor was there sound footing on this trail to that which was sought. At length a lodge was reached. Behind drawn curtains there were faint gleams of light. Four sharp knocks were given and the door opened a crack while a sentinel stepped out to examine those who craved admission. A curious passerby might have seen by

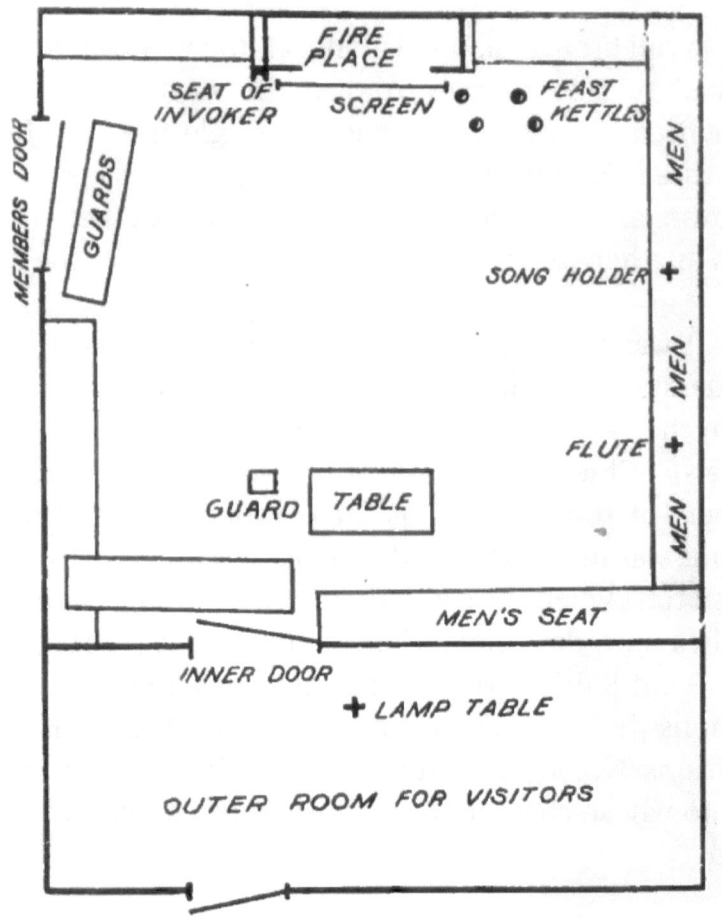

Diagram showing the form of the Lodge of the Ancient Guards of the Mystic Potence.

a hurried glance that the form of the lodge was an oblong, that there were two altars, upon one of which was placed a tray on incense and a heap of strange paraphernalia But the door soon closed, and hours afterward the sounds of a peculiar chant, the blend of wild forest sounds mingled with a strange rushing noise, like that of a great cataract, floated out from the walls of the lodge-house. What was happening within?

Is There an Undiscovered Masonry?

When the traveler or the ethnologist returns from his journey to one of the world's out-of-the-way places and comes again into the society of his friends and brothers, he finds that certain subjects are of perennial interest and that men are curious to know what he has learned of them. Not the least among these subjects is Freemasonry. It is not the Freemason alone who is curious of Freemasonry; every man who enjoys the society of his fellow men and who sees in the symbols that are found in the world about him moral lessons that admonish him to virtue also sees in all Cosmos the potentialities of Masonry. Thus, the student who has penetrated Earth's strange lands and places is called upon to tell what other races and peoples know of mystic orders that bind men to morality and brotherly devotion.

In America, we are asked what the native Red Man has of Masonry and if he has signs, grips, and words like those of the ancient craft. Often, the question comes directly: "Are American Indians Masons?" Rumors have long been afloat that there are tribes with Masonic lodges. Masons traveling amongst them have been greeted by familiar signs and words and even led into lodges where ceremonies were conducted in due form. Is it then true that in some way our ancient brethren have traveled in unknown parts and among scarcely known people and have communicated the rituals that we hold must be inviolate, or that they have issued dispensations to these veiled lodges by which they may work under competent jurisdiction? How much of Masonry do these extra-limital Masons know, and how well do they keep and conceal from the profane their secret arts? If they did not receive their Masonry from moderns, where in the annals of antiquity did they discover it?

Such are the questions directed to the traveler who has observed the customs of the outer peoples of the world. In asking such questions, the interrogator assumes more than he may rightly do, but he only desires a correct impression and the facts of the case.

What Is Freemasonry?

Let us reflect a little. Let us ask ourselves what Masonry is, for our answer to this question depends on our interpretation of extra-limital or universal Masonry.

Is Masonry only the operation of a certain ritual; is Masonry only the arbitrary practice of a rite within the walls of a lodge, without relation to conduct in the world of men? Is Masonry, in its essence, only a material act or a spiritual impulse? Suppose we admit that the spirit of Masonry lies in the practice of its moral and philosophical teachings. In that case, we may be prepared to believe that these truths may be clothed in diverse raiment and colored by varied hues, depending on the color and fragrance of rose upon the air it breathes, the water it drinks, and the soil from which it springs, as well as upon its tetrakinetic impulses. It is not the legend or the allegory that is essential in universal Freemasonry; it is the moral and the truth that is pointed out. It matters not what brings the truth to the mind and conscience so long as virtuous action follows the particular truths the rite teaches.

Let competent Masons remember where they first became Masons. Their eyes had not beheld, or their minds had not conceived the beauties of a single Masonic rite. Yet, having once seen and understood, the ritual shaped their previous beliefs, gave them a plan of action, and confirmed the power of true faith.

Masons are thus taught that there is an *inherent* Masonry in men capable of becoming Masons and that there is an *inductive* Masonry into which inherent Masons are led, to be taught the special principles of Masonry using such rites as the experience and the wisdom of our ancient brethren have deemed as truly Masonic in the accepted sense.

What Is the Natural Masonry of the Red Man?

Whether our American Indians can become Masons in their native life must be determined by examining their beliefs. Whether they have a form of inherent or natural Masonry must be determined by examining their fraternities and secret organizations. We must also make this examination to discover whether or not they have an accepted Masonry built up through the practice of the rites we observe.

The last proposition we may dismiss, for what means had the Red Man of knowing of the special rites of an order that up to 1717 was in a state of crystallization and evolution and whose lectures had not yet become fixed? A thorough examination will reveal that the Indians indeed had Freemasonry but not the Accepted Masonry. However, we may perhaps understand our Masonry better if we understand more of the Indian's Freemasonry.

First, let us examine the inherent capacity of the higher members of the various Indian tribes to receive the teachings of Masonry and their fundamental beliefs as may be in harmony with it. With the Iroquoian family of Indians, at least, the sacred number is four. We find that the Iroquois held four fundamental beliefs. Other tribes and nations of Red Men held these same truths supremely evident.

1. GOD. The Red Man believed in a Supreme Deity. Many authorities have denied this, perhaps for three reasons. Confusion of terms may have led to misunderstanding. The words that the explorer translated, *gods, spirits, and powers,* may have seemed to have precluded a Supreme God, Spirit, or Power. But, we may well believe that in some instances, at least the ignorance of the informant, the inquirer, or both led to the failure to discover a statement of a Supreme Power. And, thirdly, sad to say, in some cases, there seems to be a prejudice against admitting that natural man can know of one God to emphasize the degradation of the unregenerate. But though the native Indian spoke of spirits of nature and gods, those who were instructed by the sages of their race knew that there was one Supreme Spirit who governed and directed all others. Whether it was the *Gitche Manitou* of the Algonquin, *Tirawa* of the Pawnee, or the *Haweniu* of the Iroquois, the same idea prevailed—that of one Great Spirit. The Indian would no more think of denying the existence of a Supreme Being than he would of disputing his own existence. The first presupposed the latter; thus, with the religious leaders and the initiate, the Great Spirit was called Our Creator. The Great Architect of the Universe to the Indian was the Maker of All.

2. MORALITY. The practice of virtue was demanded of every Red Man. He must be just in his dealings with his fellows, truthful, charitable, and considerate. He must also be stoical, slow to anger, and slow to admit personal discomfort. He must always recognize his dependence upon the Maker of all and be taught to enter upon no significant undertaking without first thanking the Maker for the strength that gave him the power to perform the deed he willed. Thus, the Pawnee sang in his ritual:

What Is the Natural Masonry of the Red Man?

> Tira wa, harken! Mighty One,
> Above us in the blue, silent sky!
> We, standing, wait for thy bidding here.

The Iroquois, recognizing his helplessness without the presence of his Maker, waged his holy wars against the jealous tribes about him to bring them into the League of the Everlasting Peace. The Iroquois were assailing the forts of the Eries and calling out for a surrender. The haughty Eries yelled back in defiance, "We shall not surrender so long as our strong weapons fight for us." The Iroquois War Captain replied, "Then surrender, for it is the Master of Life who fights for us!" And the Eries went down to a shameful defeat. So, before he acts, the Iroquois chant his prayer:

> You, the All Maker,
> All high Above
> Best Friend of people;
> We ask you to help us,
> We implore your favor.

Let us not judge our Indian brethren as savages only because of what we accuse them of in war. They did shameful deeds, and these we do not forget, but why do we, with so great diligence, forget our own horrible deeds committed against the Indians—deeds that their own but weakly parallel? We, too, have sinned; through our higher ideals, all cried out for the virtues we claimed but forgot in the heat of conflict.

3. IMMORTALITY. One of the strongest beliefs of the Red Man was in a future life. Call the place of that life what you

will—the "World Beyond the Sky," the "Happy Hunting Ground," or the "Abode of the Creator"—to the Red Man, it was heaven. That present conduct would affect the future life was believed.

4. BROTHERHOOD.   Suppose there is one belief above another that affects the conduct of the Indian. In that case, it is his belief in the universal kinship of all created things. Man was not only the brother of man because a supreme Father had created both, but every animal, plant, rock, and force of nature was believed to sustain a particular relation to man. The deer and the bear were brothers and "very near man." The trees had spirits, and so did the cliffs and the waterfalls. Thus, the Red Man thought speaking to them as friends and brothers was entirely rational. No animal was killed wantonly, and every animal slain for meat or pelt was appeased by a chant asking its pardon for the deed since it had seemed a necessity for the hunter to have the meat and skin of the "brother." Then, a little sacrifice was made, incense was burned, and a gift to the spirit of the slain animal was buried beneath the ashes of the fire. To the Red Man, the earth's creatures were relatives but in a different form, as suited to the Creator's purpose, and none might be destroyed without reason and sacrifice. Even the pharmaceutical plants of the forest were not taken without an offering of thanks and the planting of the seed in the hole from which the root or stem had been pulled.

This feeling of fraternity worked out in many other ways, such as by organizing numerous fraternities and societies, knitting the clan system, and ties of a complex social organization. Some binding laws and customs governed every social action and regulated conduct. So deeply impressed was

Rodger Williams with the kindness and courteous action of the Indians among whom he lived that he wrote:

> If Nature's Sons, both wild and tame,
> Humane and courteous be:
> How ill becomes it, Sons of God
> To want Humanity?

The influence of this feeling of brotherhood made *hospitality* the universal rule among the Indians. Every stranger who came with honest intent found a welcome and a home. There was no hunger that all did not share, no feast that was not open to everyone. No orphan needs to fear the lack of home or care for his clan members provided for him. Among many tribes, the custom of having a sworn brother was observed. Each was responsible for the punishment of any encroachment or injury upon the other. Companies of these brothers often united in associations, which in no uncertain sense were fraternities.

How Did American Indian Freemasonry Originate?

Among many Indian tribes, ceremonial societies and fraternities exercised considerable influence. The Jesuits, in their missionary tours among the Hurons early in the 17th century, made note of the co-fraternities among the tribes of Canada. In later years, the publications of several learned societies and institutions have given us the records of ethnologists and anthropologists by which we learn of many native societies, associations, and fraternities. We cannot mention them all, but it would be a mistake not to call attention to the fraternities of the Zuni and other pueblo dwelling peoples. These had elaborate lodge rooms or kivas, and their altars were decorated and dedicated to the powers of nature. They taught their initiates the philosophies of their respective cults and exacted specific promises and obligations. Among the Pawnees were a number of important societies, one of the most important being the Hako. The Navahos had their cults, and the Ojibwa of the north had their Mide Wiwin. Likewise, the Iroquois had and still have their Ho-noh-che-noh-gaah, Ha-dish-dos, Society of Charm Holders, and many others.

The Indians drew moral lessons and analogies from the art of building their long houses and other dwellings in some instances, but for the most part, their symbolism was drawn from the study of the Temple of Nature. They knew of no Hebrew legends or records, and the names of Zerubbabel, Solomon, Hiram of Tyre, or Aaron were strange to them.

On the other hand, there were societies that used sacred words, some of which might be mentioned only at low breath and some never except within the lodge. Because of the secrecy and sacredness of the meaning of some words they lost their meaning and were used only because they were

The Lodge of the Eagle Society, from a drawing by Jesse Cornplanter, a Seneca artist

ancient and were supposed to be of magical value. There were many "lost words" and in some instances certain portions of the rituals were not intelligible because nearly every word was a portion of a lost ritualistic language.

There can be no doubt that certain Indian societies had secret words that their members might use in conversation or as signals. The possession of ritualistic words that belonged exclusively to the cult or fraternity was jealously guarded. With the Indians, words had a significance entirely apart from their meaning. Words were *things;* names were things. So profoundly was this doctrine taught that a man's very name could be taken from him by the proper authorities. He could likewise be forbidden to utter certain words because words and names were property and might be used or shared only by those justly entitled to receive the same.

The Masonry of the Indians as builders and philosophers dealing with moral truths grew out of their experiences with nature and with the actions of humankind. The wise men of the tribes knew that a band of men pledged to uphold morality and enact rituals that showed its advantages would constitute a dynamic influence.

Was the Red Man a Craftsman and Builder?

Except in the southwest, the Indians erected no great buildings of stone. In the northwest, especially along the coast, elaborate wooden buildings were built in the familiar log cabin style with carved pillars, posts, and heraldic devices. It is not strange to relate, perhaps, to the fact that numerous fraternities existed in these two areas where building and craftsmanship were so highly specialized. The dwellings were simpler in other regions, especially in the great plains. On the east coast and extending well into the Mississippi Valley on the eastern side, many of the Indian nations were village and town dwellers living in bark-covered houses, some of them large and roomy. The Iroquoian peoples, for example, had "long houses" built of poles, tree trunks, and bark. Their towns were surrounded by stockades of tree trunks, sometimes three rows being used. Unlike the Indians of the plains who must move as the buffalo herds moved, the East Coast Indians were more or less sedentary. They were thus able to build up a compact form of government and evolve a well-knit social organization system.

In digging into the earth where these ancient towns of the red men once arose, we discover the durable artifacts made by their craftsmen. Working only with tools of stone and bone, they made many beautiful objects, the form and symmetry of which excite the admiration and applause of modern observers. The archeological museums of America contain numerous examples of the Indian's handiwork. From these things, we learn that the native Americans of old had a keen eye, a skillful hand, and a sense of balance and harmony of form that is scarcely equaled today. Take any well-made and polished hatchet head of stone (sometimes called *celts* and often erroneously "skinning stones"). By placing it on a smooth, level surface, you will discover that it can be spun on one side, the axis being plainly visible, and the balance perfect. Here is a demonstration of a studied attempt to perfect the art of balance and symmetry.

The Indian's knowledge of form is proven by inspecting their implements. They produced polished spheres, ovoids, crescents, circles, squares, circular disks, triangles, hemispheres, pyramids, etc. In drawing geometrical designs, however, they seldom went beyond an octagon. The Indian, it will be seen, had his form of the plumb, the level, the square, and the compasses.

Some will state that the Indians never made objects that reveal craftsmanship but that such things are the work of the "mound builders." Such people are not well informed of modern research, for if they were, they would know that the mound builders were Indians and that the old-time theory of the mysterious "Mound Builders" is an exploded myth. Indians built the mounds and made all aboriginal artifacts found in them. Documents have been discovered that prove that the French and Spanish explorers saw the Indians erecting mounds. All archeological authorities now know that America had no "mysterious race that was vanquished by the Indians."

What Was the Red Man's Religious Life?

It would be interesting to trace out the various forms of religious belief held by the American natives. Still, though there are those competent to write upon this subject, it is so vast in its extent that no individual writer has yet dared the attempt. We have briefly outlined the essential features of the Indian belief, but of the numerous customs and rites, we have yet to suggest little. Perhaps an outline of the religious rites of a single nation or stock will suffice. Let us take the Iroquois.

To the Iroquois, the world was the handiwork of a Creator. He was known under various names, such as Great Ruler, Good Mind, Sky Dweller, and Creator. It was believed that life came to the earth from heaven in the form of a woman ready to give life to a girl child. Seeing a rift in the sky above, the Great Turtle of the black chaos called out to the water creatures of the darkness and told them of the event, bidding them try to bring some substance that would grow if placed upon his shell. At length, after many creatures had perished, one deposited the earthy substance on the turtle's back, and the substance grew. Then, the night birds flew upward and received the sky mother on an island formed by their interlaced wings. With great gentleness, she was placed upon the earthy back of the Turtle. As she rested, a girl child was born who grew and became mature. All was dark until the sky-mother stuck the stalk of the Flower of Light in the soil.

The firstborn then commenced to go round and round the island, finding that it became larger each time she tried the journey. One of her latter journeys took longer than others, for the island had grown very near a place called East. She paused on the shore, and a warm wind came and whispered to her. She felt it encircle her and lift her from her feet, but her heart was thrilled with a strange ecstasy. She returned to her mother's camp and told of the strange experience, but the Sky Mother only wept.

After a season, the First-Born-of-Earth gave birth to two boys, one called the Light One and the other the Dark One, who had a heart of flint. In giving birth to the twins, the mother died, leaving them to the care of the Sky Mother. The boys grew to maturity immediately and demanded to know their father. One was kind and built things; the other was ferocious and destroyed anything that came his way. The Light One received the name of Good Minded, and the evil one was called Bad Minded. Good Minded cared for his mother's grave and watered it because the Sky Mother had told him to do so. He watched over it with great devotion until he was rewarded by seeing plants spring from the grave. The tobacco came from the head, the corn from her breasts, the pumpkin from her waist, and the edible tubers and beans from her feet. Sound Mind then asked his mother where he should find his father and was told to journey to the east sea and cross to a mountain rising from the water. This, after great difficulty, he did. Standing at the mountain's base, he called, "My Father, where art thou?" And the reply came, "A Son of Mine shall cast the great cliffs from the mountain's edge to the summit of this peak." Sound Mind clasped the cliffs and flung them afar over the top of the mountain. Then came the voice, "A Son of Mine shall swim the cataract from the base to the top."

Good Minded flung himself into the merciless current and swam his way upward to the top of a ledge near the mountain top. Then again, the voice sounded, "A Son of Mine shall wrestle with the hurricane." A great wind swept about Good Minded as if to sweep him from his unstable footing. Still, he wrestled with the wind, though he could not see it or tell where to grasp it, until the hurricane cried out, "Enough for you to have exhausted my breath." Once more, the voice sounded, "A Son of Mine shall brave the fire of hottest flame. Come!" From the mountainside burst a flame that burned and blinded Good Minded, but he pushed through the twisting arms and ran up the mountain to the summit. There in repose was a being so infinitely brilliant that Good Minded could scarcely see.

"I am thy Father," said the Light, "Thou art My Son." Then the Father gave Good Mind the power to make the earth grow with all manner of plants and trees. In a package, he placed the magical dust that would become animal life. Long, the Father spoke to his Son and then bade him depart.

When Good Minded returned to Earth Island and told his Grandmother, the Sky Woman, where he had been and what power he had received, Bad Minded became very jealous and, by an ingenious plan, sought to destroy him. But after a lengthy battle, the Bad Minded was vanquished and put in a deep cavity in the earth along with all the perverted and distorted creatures he had made from the good creatures. The evil creatures were banished because they chose to be evil rather than as they had been created.

Then the Good Minded took the face of his mother and flung it into the heavens, and it became the moon. At that time, a new light far more brilliant appeared; it was the Sun. So came the Sun to rule the day and the Moon to give hope to the night.

When all things had been perfected, Good Minded looked into a pool of water and saw his own face. He took a handful of clay and molded his image, which became a man.

Many pre-humans were on the Earth then and were subdued and told their function. They were forbidden to molest men. When all this was finished, the Sky Mother said to her grandson, "We must return to the world above the sky, our Ga-o-ya-geh." So did they return to the Father, but they never watched over us, for we are their children, and because they were, we are.

Such is the Indian's Genesis, and though briefly told, there will be few who cannot see in it an incredible symbolism and an accurate recognition of man's divine origin. We observe that the last great test of the good-minded is not alone in overcoming earth and water and fire and air, which are material, but in banishing evil and all its distortions.

Through a series of religious tales such as this, the Iroquois were taught the essentials of moral life and the recognition of man's relation to his Creator. The lessons of these unwritten gospels teach Fortitude, Loyalty, Patriotism, Tolerance, Fraternity, and Gratitude.

The Iroquois were religious in every act, for they were not the Creator in all He had created. Sin, thus, became a thing that man could commit against himself, against his fellows, human and non-human, and against the interests of the tribe. It was not believed that the Creator could be sinned against, for he was above an injury by man. Nor was it possible for a sin to be forgiven for effect always followed action. What we have done, we have done, and not even divinity can say it was not done, nor can the effects be wiped away. For the guilty, there was no escape through forgiveness from the Creator. Sins against self and society must be paid for by restitution in some form.

There were many religious ceremonies for the Iroquois. Still, the grand ceremonies were those for seasonal thanksgiving, of which there were six each year. Gratitude to the Creator was the underlying principle of the Red Man's religion. One of the stanzas in the Thanksgiving rite is:

For all that He has Created, we should offer thanks,
For all the things from below up to himself in the sky-world,
We who are here gathered in assembly thank our Creator—
Yea, all his creatures who are living here in this earth-world.

Most of the members of the various Iroquois tribes — the Seneca, the Cayuga, the Onondaga, the Oneida, and the Mohawk are now Christians, living as white men do. But so remarkable a hold have their ancestors' old rites and religion upon some that the old beliefs still hold among a considerable portion of the Onondagas and Senecas in New York state and Canada.

The Senecas of the old belief hold their religious rites in their Long Houses, the Temples of their Faith. Here, the honest student may observe these rites and determine whether a person whose religious heritage is what we have described may be called "pagan" or not. Is there not something racially heroic in this stand of the Senecas to preserve that which is distinctive of their people? Yet, slowly but surely, the old life is fading, and in time, it will all be gone. The Senecas will have succumbed to the heat of the melting pot.

Sentinel of the Society of False Faces The False Face Company is one of the most spectacular of the Iroquois.

WHAT HAPPENED?

What you have read in these pages was told to a great Mason, long before he made his journey to the land of the Senecas and witnessed their ceremonies. The Senecas called him Ho-doin-jai-ey, the Holder of the Earth, and they invited Ho-doin-jai-ey to come as a novitiate to the Lodge of the Ancient Guards of the Mystic Potence. Two other friends of the Senecas had been invited; Ho-skwi-sa-oh and Ga-jee-wa, thus forming the mystic triangle.

Red Hand, The Brother-Friend

The candidates were told to listen. The legend of the Ancient Guards was told. The complete story would make a lengthy document, though I am sure you would find it a marvelous tale.

Red Hand was a young chief whose life was blameless, for he was Ho-ya-di-wa-doh. He had received certain mysterious knowledge that made the covetous envy him. Still, Red Hand was so brave and kind that men and warriors admired and loved him.

Red Hand had a place where he spoke to the Great Mystery. Because the Great Mystery spoke to him, he was kind to every brother of the earth —every tree, every rock, every animal. He fed the hungry birds in wintertime. When the wolves were hungry, he gave them meat; when the deer were hungry, he gave them grass and moss. The children loved him because he gave them trinkets; the old people were grateful to him because he knew of oils that cured their lameness; the warriors admired him because he had the power to lead them against the enemy that sought to destroy them.

Down to the south country in the valley of Ohio, a war party was formed to punish the foe. The Leader went apart to seek the chief of the enemy, and while he stood alone, a poisoned arrow struck him, and he fell. Then, the assassin who rushed upon him demanded the secret of his power, but he would not give it. So the enemy lifted his tomahawk and scalped our Leader, taking the scalp away in triumph to be dried over the lodge poles where the smoke issues forth.

A wolf lifted his nose and smelled blood. He howled to bring the pack and followed the scent to the body of a man. He saw it was Brother Friend, whom he knew as Red Hand. He called in a different sound, and there came all the chiefs of the animals and even the chiefs of all the great plants and trees. They looked at the body of their friend. Then, they held a council as to how he should be revived. "We will give the tip of our hearts and the spark from our brains," they said. Then they sent for the scalp the Dew Eagle brought, making it alive again by sprinkling it from the pool of dew resting on his back. It was placed on the crown of Red Hand's head and grew fast.

One by one, the greatest of created things gave up the vital parts of their beings, the tips of their hearts, and the hearts of their brains. A brother is not a friend if he will not give his life to the brother friend who has helped him in a great emergency. When the life sparks were reduced to dust, so small a quantity was there that there was only enough to fill an acorn cup. Then, the other chiefs of the animals, trees, plants, and birds gathered around while the wolf took a cup of bark and, dipping it with the current of a spring, dropped three tiny grains of the dust of life into the water. This water of life was poured into the mouth of Red Hand, and he moved. A compress of the water healed his wounds. Then, the chosen band commenced chanting the Ancient Guardians of the Mystic Potence ritual. During the night of blackness, they sang, reciting the life and adventures of Red Hand. He awoke but lay still with his eyes shut. He listened and learned the song. The eagles' wings lifted him and bore him to a great waterfall. He heard the rushing of strong waters thundering down upon the craigs below.

Red Hand, The Brother-Friend

The whippoorwill called, and a light floated over the darkness.

Then the circle clustered closer, and the brother, the Bear, touched the breast of Red Hand. All stood erect. The Bear grasped the hand of the Leader who was to be raised, though slain. The Bear grasped his hand and, by a strong grip, raised Red Hand to his feet. All was darkness, but Red Hand lived. * * * *

The Ancient Guards called, each with his own peculiar cry. Red Hand recognized his friends. * * * *

Yiewanoh, who has passed through the initiation of the Ancient Guards, tells us the story of Red Hand.

It is a night of darkness impenetrable. There is no sound save the waterfall and the river. In the forest, the leader, patient and listening, awaits the sign promised to him. Will it be given? Yes, for the Birds and Beasts do not lie!

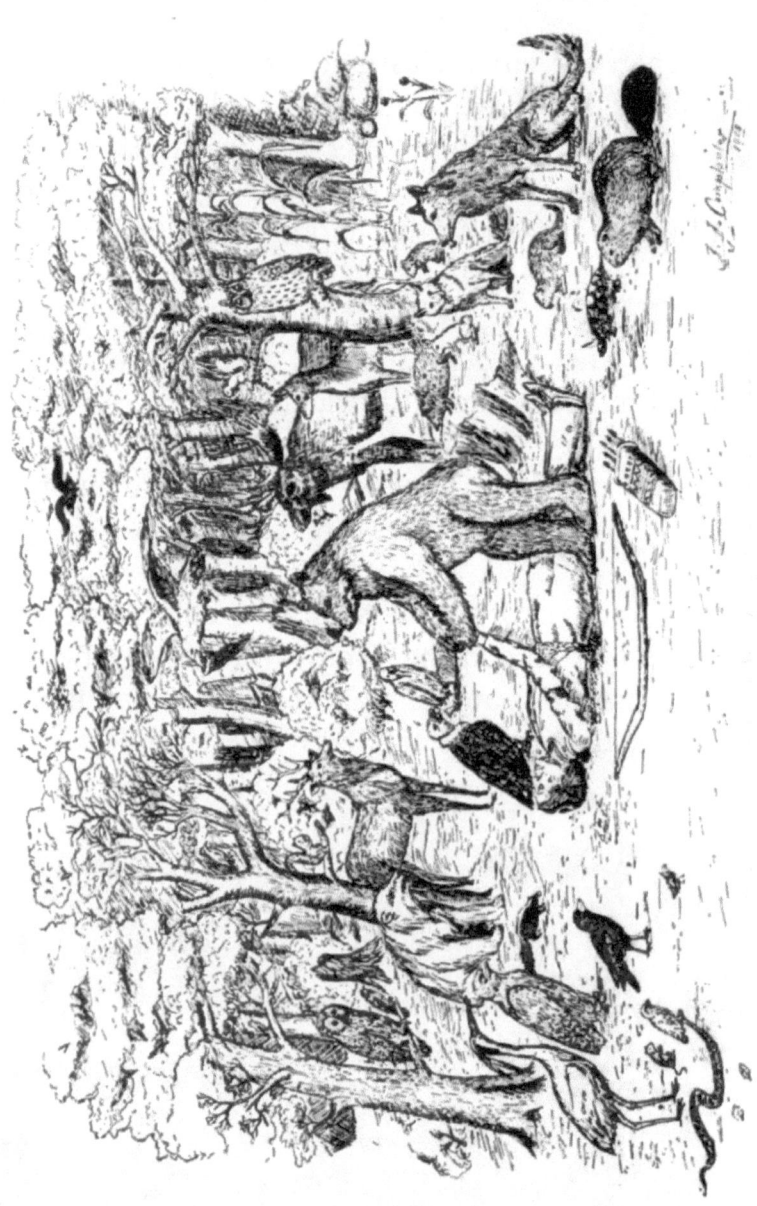

The animal council raising to life the founder of the Little Water Society

The Promise of Power

The Leader, who is Red Hand, trusts and waits until a strong voice from the darkness comes, saying:

"Hast thou cleansed thyself from human guilt and impurity?"

"I have," Red Hand replied.

"Hast thou ill will toward any of thy fellow creatures?"

"I have not."

"Wilt thou trust and obey us, keeping thyself always chaste and valorous?"

"I will."

"Wilt thou hold this power with which we endow thee for thine own chosen company only?"

"I will."

"Wilt thou endure death or torture in its cause?"

"I will."

"Wilt thou vow this secret never to be revealed save at thy death hour?"

"I will."   * * * *

"Thy death hour will be revealed to thee; thou wilt be allowed to choose thy successor, and at the end of thy journey, thou wilt be rewarded for faith and obedience."   * * * *

There was a rushing wind, and the sound of hurrying creatures was heard. The song was renewed, and then a winged light appeared. The voices were bidding him journey on.

So sings the whippoorwill, "Follow me, follow me,"

So replies the Chief to him, "Yes, I will follow thee."

"See, the night is darkening; the shadows are hiding.

No light to follow now," so sings the waterfall.

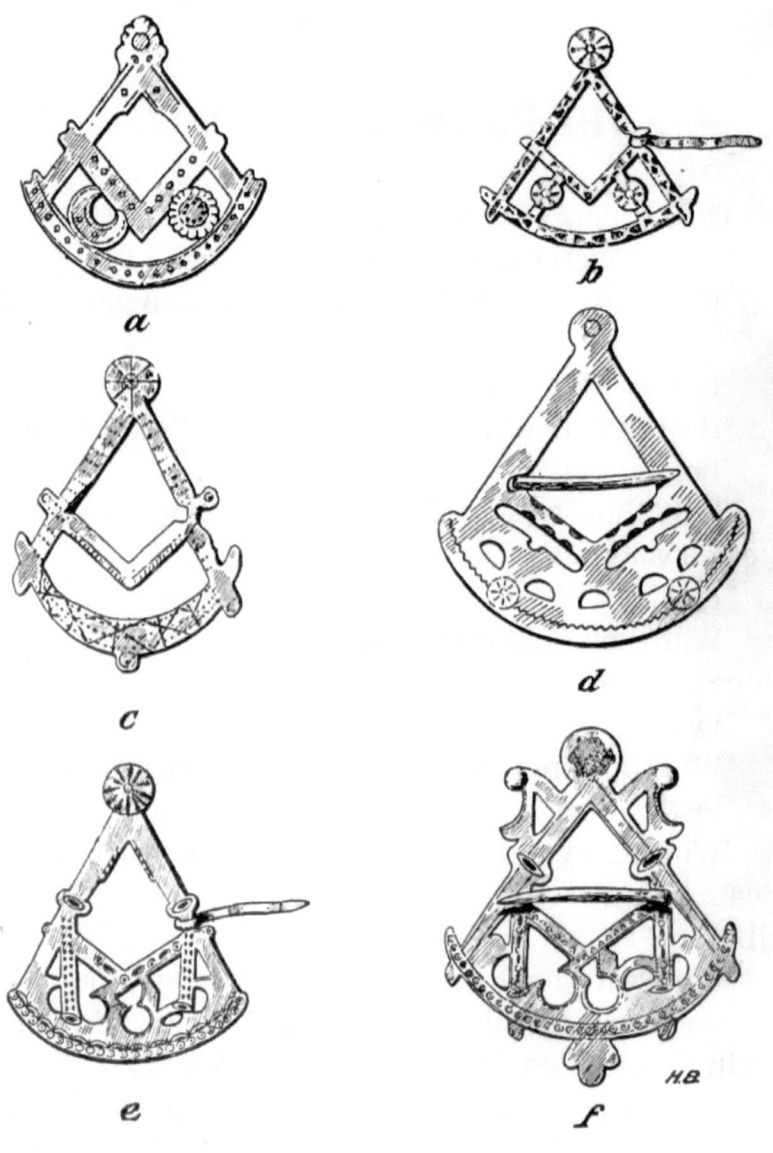

Forms of ceremonial and decorative brooches of silver, used by the Seneca Indians. Red Jacket wore the brooch marked a.

Down the deep abyss went Red Hand, following his unseen guide. He felt the waterfall's spray and climbed up until he knew he was ascending a mountain. The dawn light appeared, and he went on and on until the sun was high, when he found the flat summit of the hill.

A wild maize plant was in the circle of an altar. At its roots was the box holding the mystic potency that restores men to live and heal wounds.

A white flint knife lay at the roots of the maize plant, and a voice called, "Slash into the stalk of the Maize!" Our Leader cut the stalk, and blood flowed from the wound. Then again, a voice said, "Touch the wound with the potency." He did this, and the wound immediately healed. The voice sounded again, saying:

"Guard well this mystic potency for while ye have it, thy people shall endure. When it is gone, they shall be no more. Go and found an order that shall know all this wisdom and preserve in the bonds of faithful brotherhood the mysteries, the chants, and the will to perform the task of spreading the knowledge of the kinship of all created things."

* * * *

Da neho enyayehak.

* * * *

Out of the Darkness

The Order has been founded, and though many centuries have passed, the faithful fraternity remains. The members impersonate the brother-friends who gave their lives in the ritual. In the mystic square in the darkness, we hear their voices. The call of the birds is heard, and the shrill call of the Guide bird comes toward morning to herald the promise of the day. The waters thunder with a deafening sound—and so deeply do these sounds imbed themselves into the memory of the ears that it is days before they are forgotten.

The lights appear during the night intervals at three periods, and the Brothers refresh themselves with berry juice mixed with maple sugar. The sacred incense of the O-yan-kwa is burned. The altars are covered when the light appears.

The morning song comes at last with the calling of great flocks of crows. Then appears the boar's head or perhaps that of a bear, steaming with the fragrant soup of the maize. There is a ceremonial partaking of the feast, and then the O-noh-kwa is distributed. It is just before dawn, and the company has adjourned. The session has been from the beginning of total darkness until its end.

The lodge of Neh Ho-noh-chee-noh-ga has been closed; the Ancient Guards of the Mystic Potence gather up their mystery bundles that hold the sacred Ni-ga-ni-gaa-ah. * * * * It is still night though the Ga-no-dah * * * * has been ended.
We wait in the darkness. Come all ye who listen!

Out of the Darkness

Help us in our dark journey, now no sun is shining;
Now, no star is glowing. Come show us the pathway!
The night is not friendly; she closes her eyelids;
The moon has forgotten us; we wait in the darkness.
"Follow me, follow me,"—so sings the whippoorwill.
"Yes, I am following," so the Chief answers him!

****

DA-NE-HOH. WHAT HAS HAPPENED HAS HAPPENED.

A tall bronze-skinned guide led the way over an ice-rutted road. The journey from the mysterious East had commenced. Following the Guide in a single file were four and there were four. It was the land of the Senecas, the most powerful confederates of the Six Nations of the Iroquois. To this land in the Valley of the Cattaraugus had journeyed the Commander-in-Chief of Buffalo Consistory and three other members of the Ancient Accepted Scottish Rite of Masonry. Now, they were on their way back to the city that rises where the ancient Seneca town of Do-sho-we once had its site. These pale-faced members of the race that came and possessed the red man's land had been adopted brothers and initiated into the highest rites of the Senecas.

Little has been told; the door has only been held ajar in the slightest space, and no secrets have been revealed. There were feather wands and deer skins but no purple robes or crowns. Yet, who shall say that the Senecas do not have the thread of the legend of Osiris or that they do not have an inherent Freemasonry?

Egyptian diagram of the raising of Osiris

*Da-Ne-Hoh. What Has Happened
Has Happened.*

The Three Initiates in the Ancient Guards of the Mystic Potence

*George L. Tucker   George K. Staples   Everett R. Burmrster
(Ho-skwi-sa-onh)   (Ho-doin-djai-ey)   (Ga-je-wa)*

A Practical Postscript

Our knowledge of remote antiquity is derived not so much from the traditions handed down by the ancients as from the enduring relics of craftsmanship that have survived. It was the poet Bryant who wrote:

> The forms they hewed from living stone
> Survive the waste of years alone
> And mingled with their ashes, show
> What greatness perished long ago.

In the halls of the Buffalo Consistory, A.A.S.R. is a splendid collection of Indian artifacts collected from the ancient forts, village sites, and burial places of the Indians who lived in western New York from early to recent times. This collection, brought together through the unceasing efforts of George L. Tucker, constitutes a museum of antiquity and illustrates the handiwork of the American Indians. It has grown under the patronage of George K. Staples, who has looked with sympathy for its development. Everett R. Burmaster of Irving, N.Y., a field archaeologist of rare ability and insight, added many fine specimens to this collection. Today, the Tucker Collection is sought by archaeologists and studied because of its interesting and unique character.

There is an intimate connection between archaeology and Masonry. The archaeologist finds the lost cornerstones of history and, with his trowel, unearths records that history has failed to write. The archaeologist gives us new knowledge of our ancient brethren wherever they were distributed over the earth. The archaeologist points out the basic lessons of history, for he alone has explored the sub-cellars of the temple of civilization.

Every relic found on the sites where the primitive peoples of the world once lived is a lost letter, syllable, or word. The archaeologist combines these parts and is able to interpret the lost story of tribes and races.

It is most fitting to have a collection of ancient artifacts in the Buffalo Consistory. It gives the members a rare opportunity to read about life and understand the thoughts of ancient man. The collection should grow, and every friend of science should feel it a privilege to make the collection grow. I can think of no better way for this to be done than by depositing in the archives of this museum some stone-built substance as a memorial that we of today feel our appreciation of a stalwart effort to create a memorial to the craftsmen of past ages. Every man and Mason who places a stone into this Foundation assists in building an actual temple wherein the truths that antiquity has left as our inheritance will be preserved. We who have the fragments of missing history have this opportunity. It is a Masonic opportunity for the writer, as a student of anthropology, to respectfully invite your interest.

If this call is rightly received and there is a real response, there is no reason why Buffalo should not have a Masonic Museum of Archaeology and History. This museum would be worthy of Masonry in Buffalo and would afford students a Mecca where they may receive more light.

ARTHUR C. PARKER.

GA-WA-SO-WA-NEH
Arthur C. Parker

Thank you for buying this Cornerstone book!

For over 25 years now, I've tried to provide the Masonic community with quality books on Masonic education, philosophy, and general interest. Your support means everything to us and keeps us afloat. Cornerstone is by no means a large company. We are a small family-owned operation that depends on your support.

Please visit our website and have a look at the many books we offer as well as the different categories of books.

If your lodge, Grand Lodge, research lodge, book club, or other body would like to have quality Cornerstone books to sell or distribute, write us. We can give you outstanding books, prices, and service.

Thanks again!
Michael R. Poll
Publisher

Cornerstone Book Publishers
1cornerstonebooks@gmail.com
http://cornerstonepublishers.com

More Masonic Books from Cornerstone

Living Freemasonry
A Better Path to Travel
by Michael R. Poll
6x9 Softcover 180 pages
ISBN 99781934935958

The Particular Nature of Freemasons
by Michael R. Poll
6x9 Softcover 156 pages
ISBN 9781613423462

10,000 Famous Freemasons
4 Vol. Softcover Edition
by William Denslow
Foreword by Harry S. Truman
Cornerstone Foreword by Michael R. Poll
8.5 x 11, Softcover 2 Volumes 1,515 pages
ISBN 1887560319

Historical Inquiry into the Origins of the Ancient and Accepted Scottish Rite
by James Foulhouze
Edited by Jonathan K. Poll
Foreword by Michael R. Poll
6×9 Softcover 288 pages
ISBN: 978-1-61342-026-3

The Scottish Rite Papers
A Study of the Troubled History of the Louisiana and US Scottish Rite in the Early to Mid-1800s
by Michael R. Poll
6x9 Softcover 240 pages
ISBN 9781613423448

Cornerstone Book Publishers
www.cornerstonepublishers.com

More Masonic Books from Cornerstone

Alchemist in a Masonic Apron
A Masonic Book for Freemasons During Their Evolution
By Michael R. Poll
6×9 Softcover 176 pages
ISBN: 978-1-61342-498-8

Seeking Light
The Esoteric Heart of Freemasonry
by Michael R. Poll
6×9 Softcover 156 pages
ISBN: 1613422571

Measured Expectations
The Challenges of Today's Freemasonry
by Michael R. Poll
6×9 Softcover 180 pages
ISBN: 978-1613422946

A Masonic Evolution
The New World of Freemasonry
by Michael R. Poll
6×9 Softcover 176 pages
ISBN: 978-1-61342-315-8

An Encyclopedia of Freemasonry
by Albert Mackey
Revised by William J. Hughan and Edward L. Hawkins
Foreword by Michael R. Poll
8.5 x 11, Softcover 2 Volumes 960 pages
ISBN 1613422520

Cornerstone Book Publishers
www.cornerstonepublishers.com

More Masonic Books from Cornerstone

History of the Order of the Eastern Star
by Mrs. Jean M'Kee Kenaston
Restored and Edited by Jonathan K. Poll
6 x 9 Softcover 440 pages
ISBN 978-1-61342-700-2

Masonic Initiation
by W. L. Wilmshurst
Edited and Foreword by Michael R. Poll
6x9 Softcover 212 pages
ISBN 978-1-61342-446-9

Ancient Manuscripts of the Freemasons
The Transformation from Operative to Speculative Freemasonry
Edited by Michael R. Poll
6 x 9 Softcover 164 pages
ISBN: 1934935603

The Mosaic Book of the American Adoptive Rite
The Birth of the Eastern Star
by Rob Morris
Introduction by Michael R. Poll
6 x 9 Softcover 190 pages
ISBN 978-1-61342-316-5

Outline of the Rise and Progress of Freemasonry in Louisiana
by James B. Scot
Introduction by Alain Bernheim
Afterword by Michael R. Poll
Edited by Robert L. Poll
6 x 9 Softcover 315 pages
ISBN 978-1-61342-434-6

Cornerstone Book Publishers
www.cornerstonepublishers.com

More Masonic Books from Cornerstone

Masonic Enlightenment
The Philosophy, History and Wisdom of Freemasonry
Edited by Michael R. Poll
6 x 9 Softcover 180 pages
ISBN 1887560750

The Bonseigneur Rituals
A Rare Collection of 18th Century New Orleans Ecossais Rituals
Edited by Gerry L. Prinsen
Foreword by Michael R. Poll
8x10 Softcover 2 volumes 574 pages
ISBN 1934935344

Our Stations and Places - Masonic Officer's Handbook
by Henry G. Meacham
Revised by Michael R. Poll
6 x 9 Softcover 164 pages
ISBN: 1887560637

Knights & Freemasons: The Birth of Modern Freemasonry
By Albert Pike & Albert Mackey
Edited by Michael R. Poll
Foreword by S. Brent Morris
6 x 9 Softcover 178 pages
ISBN 1887560661

Robert's Rules of Order: Masonic Edition
Revised by Michael R. Poll
6 x 9 Softcover 212 pages
ISBN 1887560076

Cornerstone Book Publishers
www.cornerstonepublishers.com

New Orleans Scottish Rite College
www.youtube.com/c/NewOrleansScottishRiteCollege

Clear, Easy to Watch
Scottish Rite and Craft Lodge
Video Education

www.ingramcontent.com/pod-product-compliance
Lightning Source LLC
LaVergne TN
LVHW041714060526
838201LV00043B/734